I'm Single, So What!

"GOD IS IN LOVE WITH ME"
NO MATTER WHAT

Table of Contents

Introduction 1

Chapter 1
I'm Single, So What!............................. 7

Chapter 2
The Six Stages of a Relationship 34

Chapter 3
It's All About the Benjamins 68

Chapter 4
The Protocol, The Promise and The
Peace 77

Chapter 5
Frequently Asked Questions 103

About the Author 123

Introduction

Let me start by saying that being single is not a debilitating disease. Being single does not diminish your value as a person. In the eyes of God, you are still His child, and He loves you very much. However, if you have not decided that you no longer want to live by ungodly standards, right now is the appointed time to receive God into your life through Jesus Christ, our Lord (Romans 10:9-10). What follows in this book is written from a biblical and practical perspective. If marriage is in God's plan for you, it will happen in His timing. Therefore, getting your priorities aligned and moving forward from the perspective of trusting Him is essential. In Matthew 6:33 (KJV), Jesus says, "But seek ye first the Kingdom of God, and his righteousness; and all these things shall be added unto you."

Regardless of our marital status, God must be first in our lives. Everything else will fall into place when you understand God's promises to you. Therefore, God should be the priority and nothing else because He keeps His word. So, if you are not seeking Him with all your heart, then you will never know the joy God has in store for you (P alms 5:11). Please do not focus on the statistics about the marriage. Some may cause you to become fearful and apprehensive about your future.

For example, the 2020 U.S. Census reported that there are 258.3 million people over 18 years old. In addition, 117.6 million Americans, ages 18 and older, single. That is 45.5 percent of the adult population.

Yet, couples who worship together regularly have less than a 10 percent divorce rate. Thus, we see the power of God in Marriage. The whole picture becomes even grimmer when you hear that the average length of a marriage is eight years. You do not have to look far to see the breakdown in our society. Just look at the status of our marriages. Our social institutions come from our marriages, the family, the church, the school, and the government. Thus, if you destroy marriage, which is the building block of society, you will ultimately ruin our local communities, as we know it to be.

Please do not focus on the statistics about the marriage. Some may cause you to become fearful and apprehensive about your future. For example, the 2020 U.S. Census reported that there are 258.3 million people over 18 years old. In addition, 117.6 million Americans, ages 18 and older, single. That is 45.5 percent of the adult population.

The divorce rate in America is also interesting. Towards the end of the last century, for first-time marriages, the divorce rate was 50 to 58 percent. The divorce rate was as high as 95 percent for those married three or more times. But for first time marriages, the divorce rate has dropped to 41 percent.

We can extrapolate the main reasons for this decline is that over the last five or so decades. The marriage rate in this country has dropped by 60 percent. Even though there are still codified benefits, the formal benefits of marriage have greatly diminished. On average, for every nuptial there are three divorces. The first-time marriages end by the eighth year.

Getting married should not be the end game – you will be single for most of your life. Instead, it would help you to focus on being your best. The secular world now recognizes the benefits of being married. Numerous studies have found that marriage increases health, longevity, quality of life, and wealth. In addition, the Bible states in Hebrews 13:4, "Marriage is honorable among all, and the bed undefiled; but fornicators and adulterers God will judge."

In this book, my target audience is single women who have never been married and have no children. Before you tune me out, the principles found in this book apply to everybody. They apply to those who are single again, single mothers, widowed, and senior singles. The principles found in the following pages come from the Holy Word of God. Thus, your prayers have been answered if you are a man or woman of faith seeking guidance or direction regarding being single!

As a Christian, I come from the biblical perspective that Jesus Christ is the center of my life (Psalm 119:105). I gave my life to Christ in August of 1972, so I am not coming from a novice point of view. I have experience, and I know that God keeps His Word. Therefore, this information is biblically based. Modern trends do not influence my convictions regarding being single, saved, and satisfied. Neither is the latest secular research or the opinions of some unsaved person. They are good to know and be aware of, but as Martin Luther said, "Sola scriptura - all truth necessary for our salvation and spiritual life is taught either explicitly or implicitly in Scripture." The Bible is the source of my information and inspiration. If you are tired of beating your head against the wall, I invite you to join me in learning more about what God has to say.

Finally, I am also coming from the biblical perspective that God expects the man to be his family's Prophet, Priest, Protector, and Provider. The man comes from a different point of view than the single woman. I have found that a woman is not married because the right person has not asked her. Women are only attracted to a certain kind of man, whereas men will fall for any beautiful woman. A man must humble himself to get married. Why would a man settle for one woman when he could have hundreds or thousands of women? A saved man's first objective should be to please his Heavenly Father. Thus, as Solomon states in Proverbs 18:22, "A man that finds a wife, finds a good thing and obtains favor from the Lord."

The man should do the pursuing, not the woman. Therefore, single women must stay in their place and live biblically, according to the Word of God! I will elaborate more on this in the following chapters. I know what the world's system tells women, but I encourage women to stay in their place and let the man pursue them. If you want godly results, you must do it God's way (Proverbs 3:5-6)!

Chapter 1
I'm Single, So What!

The main difference between single people and married people is that single people are not married, and married people are not single!

Being single does not mean that you are a second-class citizen, nor does it mean that something is wrong with you. Keep in mind that God loves you regardless of your marital status! Marriage is not for children. In 1 Corinthians 7:35, Paul says, "I am saying this for your own good, not to restrict you, but that you may live in a right way in undivided devotion to the Lord."

When Paul wrote 1 Corinthians, he believed that Jesus could return at any moment; he taught his disciples that we must be free from the entanglements of this world! And we must still live as if Jesus is coming back today because one day He will! This is the blessed hope of every believer. The following scriptures affirm our future as believers. Highlight words or phrases that resonate with you.

Scripture References:

John 14:1-6 (KJV) - Let not your heart be troubled: ye believe in God, believe also in me. [2] In my Father's house are many mansions: if it were not so, I would have told you. I go to prepare a place for you. [3] And if I go and prepare a place for you, I will come again, and receive you unto myself; that where I am, there ye may be also. [4] And whither I go ye know, and the way ye know. [5] Thomas saith unto him, Lord, we know not whither thou goest; and how can we know the way? [6] Jesus saith unto him, I am the way, the truth, and the life: no man cometh unto the Father, but by me."

1 Corinthians 15:51-58 (KJV) – "Behold, I shew you a mystery; We shall not all sleep, but we shall all be changed, [52] In a moment, in the twinkling of an eye, at the last trump: for the trumpet shall sound, and the dead shall be raised incorruptible, and we shall be changed. [53] For this corruptible must put on incorruption, and this mortal must put on immortality. [54] So when this corruptible shall have put on incorruption, and this mortal shall have put on immortality, then shall be brought to pass the saying that is written, Death is swallowed up in victory. [55] O death,

where is thy sting? O grave, where is thy victory? [56] The sting of death is sin; and the strength of sin is the law. [57] But thanks be to God, which giveth us the victory through our Lord Jesus Christ. 58 Therefore, my beloved brethren, be ye steadfast, unmovable, always abounding in the work of the Lord, forasmuch as ye know that your labor is not in vain in the Lord."

1 Thessalonians 4:13-18 (KJV) – "But I would not have you to be ignorant, brethren, concerning them which are asleep, that ye sorrow not, even as others which have no hope. [14] For if we believe that Jesus died and rose again, even so them also which sleep in Jesus will God bring with him. [15] For this we say unto you by the word of the Lord, that we which are alive and remain unto the coming of the Lord shall not prevent them which are asleep. [16] For the Lord himself shall descend from Heaven with a shout, with the voice of the archangel, and with the trump of God: and the dead in Christ shall rise first: [17] Then we which are alive and remain shall be caught up together with them in the clouds, to meet the Lord in the air: and so, shall we ever be with the Lord. [18] Wherefore comfort one another with these words."

1 Corinthians 6:13 (KJV) – "Meats for the belly, and the belly for meats: but God shall destroy both it and them. Now the body is not for fornication, but for the Lord, and the Lord for the body."

1 Corinthians 6:20 (KJV) - 20 "For ye are bought with a price: therefore, glorify God in your body, and in your Spirit, which are God's."

1 Corinthians 7:1-9 (KJV) – "Now concerning the things whereof ye wrote unto me: It is good for a man not to touch a woman. 2 Nevertheless, to avoid fornication, let every man have his own wife, and let every woman have her own husband. ³ Let the husband render unto the wife due benevolence: and likewise, also the wife unto the husband. ⁴ The wife hath not power of her own body, but the husband: and likewise, also the husband hath not power of his own body, but the wife. ⁵ Defraud ye not one the other, except it be with consent for a time, that ye may give yourselves to fasting and prayer; and come together again, that Satan tempt you not for your incontinency. ⁶ But I speak this by permission, and not of commandment. 7 For I would that all men were even as I myself. But every man hath his proper gift of God, one after this manner,

and another after that. 8 I say therefore to the unmarried and widows, it is good for them if they abide even as I. 9 But if they cannot contain, let them marry: for it is better to marry than to burn."

Intimacy with God

Let me reiterate that everything begins with our relationship with God through Jesus Christ, our Lord. So, Jesus told Nicodemus in John 3:3, "Jesus answered and said unto him, verily, verily, I say unto thee, except a man be born again, he cannot see the Kingdom of God." You must choose a lifestyle of righteousness and obedience to the Word of God in every area of your life. 1 Corinthians 6:14 states, "Be not unequally yoked together with unbelievers, for what fellowship has righteousness with unrighteousness? And what communion hath light with darkness?" The individuals that you surround yourself with have to be like minded especially in the areas of dating and marriage.

My focus here is on being single, never married, and having no children. My advice to single parents, especially single mothers, is to wait until your children complete high school before entering a relationship with a man. I strongly recommend this, especially if you are raising boys and/or teenagers. To me, the whole process of step-parenting is no joke! Yet it can be done and done well but know that this will not be easy! When both spouses have children from previous marriages or relationships, this marriage has a divorce rate of 70%. When Jesus Christ and His Kingdom here on earth as it is in heaven, the primary focus for Christian singles shifts from scarcity to abundance. And odds like these become God's blessings ever working in your favor.

Scripture References:

Matthew 6:33 (KJV) – "But seek ye first the Kingdom of God, and his righteousness; and all these things shall be added unto you."

It is also essential for single individuals to have a person that has wisdom, time, expertise, and biblical knowledge in their lives. These individuals are invaluable when it comes to having accountability. These individuals pass on their traits and tendencies in the areas of leadership, planning, and assessment. For example, in the Bible, Timothy was taught by Paul, Joshua was mentored by Moses, and Ruth followed Naomi.

In addition, you need someone, an older and wiser believer who has proven himself or herself honest, trustworthy, and faithful in following Christ's teachings and applying them in their daily lives. In Titus 2: 1-5 it states, "1 But as for you, speak the things which are proper for sound doctrine: 2 that the older men be sober, reverent, temperate, sound in faith, in love, in patience; 3 the older women likewise, that they be reverent in behavior, not slanderers, not given to much wine, teachers of good things— 4 that they admonish the young women to love their husbands, to love their children, 5 to be discreet, chaste, homemakers, good, obedient to their own husbands, that the word of God may not be blasphemed."

Scripture References:

Proverbs 11:14 (KJV) - Where no counsel is, the people fall: but in the multitude of counsellors there is safety.

Proverbs 15:22 (KJV) - Without counsel purposes are disappointed: but in the multitude of counsellors, they are established.

Proverbs 24:6 (KJV) - For by wise counsel thou shalt make thy war: and in multitude of counsellors there is safety.

You may be wondering; how should a Christian man pursue a Christian woman? It should be done like everything else, with prayer and fasting first. The man must truly desire a committed relationship with this woman. The purpose of prayer and fasting is for strength, courage, and purpose. What are the reasons of the pursuit? Is it marriage, or is it sex? There is a difference. Once a man identifies a lady he wants to pursue, the man should observe her for several months before making his initial contact.

The man will discover the depth of her faithfulness and if she is single during this time. He will also learn how devout she is to God and to the local church. When the man has been in prayer and observed her for several months, he can proceed and appropriately make contact. Try asking for her telephone number so you can speak with her privately. And if she desires to share her contact information, thank her, and resist the urge to want to see her immediately or communicate with her insistently. When it comes to social media, you could like her posts but comment infrequently.   You could compliment her or 13 engage in an interactive way. Direct messaging (DM) is not a substitute for verbal communication. Plan for your phone calls to be consistent. Use them for planning to meet up with church group outings or sitting together during worship or sharing about your day. The phone calls might need to start off at 10 minutes then incrementally increase by five minutes longer each month of consistent talking on the phone. The aim is to learn as much as you can about her likes, preferences, and availability.

The purpose is to spend face to face time with each other. Seek public and daylight hour activities to keep boundaries solid to protect against sexual temptation. If at any point she does not seem interested in you or your intentions, move on! Dating must always be for marriage, not for fun, because your date could be your mate, and your mate will determine your fate! In I Cor. 10:13 it reads "No temptation has overtaken you except such as is common to man; but God is faithful, who will not allow you to be tempted beyond what you are able, but with the temptation will also make the way of escape, that you may be able to bear it."

Why is it dangerous to engage in sexual activity outside of marriage? First, it is a sin. In the English Standard Version of the Bible Exodus 22:16-17 reads "If a man seduces a virgin who is not betrothed and lies with her, he shall give the bride-price for her and make her his wife. 17 If her father utterly refuses to give her to him, he shall pay money equal to the bride-price for virgins." This passage is a biblical law that deals financially with a man who sexually pressures an unmarried virgin.

It states that if a man seduces an unmarried virgin and is successful in having sexual intercourse with her, he must pay the bride-price and marry her. If the father of the virgin refuses to give her in marriage to the seducer, he must still pay the bride-price for virgins. This price is more than a meal and a movie. This was an investment in that young man's future. His respect in the community depended on him choosing early and wisely.

This law was meant to protect the honor and dignity of unmarried women, as well as to ensure that they were not left without the prospects of a husband or financial support in the event of seduction which could lead to pregnancy. It also served to discourage men from taking advantage of vulnerable women.

Secondly, there are consequences, one of which is sin (1 Corinthians 6:18) "18 Flee fornication. Every sin that a man doeth is without the body; but he that committed fornication sinneth against his own body." Engaging in sexual activity outside of marriage also brings shame and remorse, unwanted pregnancy, and the spread of sexually transmitted diseases. Fornication and its fallout are like taking a piece of gum unwrapping it then chewing it. Then passing it to someone else who continues to chew for five minutes then passing it around for others to chew. That would be gross.

Single and Satisfied or Single and Terrified!

There is a difference between a wedding and a marriage. The wedding ceremony takes less than 10 minutes, but it takes a lifetime to build a marriage. Some women love the idea of a wedding ceremony but not marriage. Some men are in love with the concept of the honeymoon but not the responsibility of marriage.

There is a story of a Pastor visiting a fourth-grade Sunday school class to discuss marriage as part of his teaching. He asked the class, "What does God say about marriage?"

Immediately one boy raised his hand and replied, "Father, forgive them, for they know not what they do." This is a little humor to bring home the terror of the statistical data, the extortion like child support demands, and the selfishness of irreconcilable differences.

Generally, a woman is not married because the right guy has not asked her. Most single women have a list of men they want to marry, and if one of those men asked her, she would gladly say "Yes!" But a man must humble himself to ask a woman to marry him. Why should he settle for one woman when he could have many women?

Valerie Clayton's book, Victory in Singleness, states, "So many women believe that Marriage is the solution to wholeness. It is not!" It takes two single people choosing to be 100 percent into the marriage. Showing up as their true and authentic selves. The original design for marriage was not to meet our fundamental emotional needs nor to fill a spiritual void – only God can do that. It is also your personal responsibility not your mate's responsibility. Yet, we entangle ourselves this way in unhealthy relationships because singleness is viewed as undesirable. The latest survey revealed that 62 percent of black women are single. A lot of quiet desperation is going on in the lives of many single, saved black women. What does this mean for the future of black marriages? Is this giving rise to many dilemmas in the black community? What will be the position of the local churches?

In the book, The Rock on Which the Family Is Built, William May said, "How depressing it can be to witness the blessing of another." How many bride's maid dresses do you have in your closet? How many weddings have you been invited to? How many girlfriends regale you with stories of their latest male interest? How many romantic comedies make up your top ten favorite movies? You could feel something like humiliation, shame even jealousy.

We belong to God (1 Corinthians 6:13-20) "Food is meant for the stomach and the stomach for food"—and God will destroy both one and the other. The body is not meant for sexual immorality, but for the Lord, and the Lord for the body." The first part of the passage is a statement about the purpose of food and the stomach - that food is meant to be consumed by the stomach and the stomach is meant to digest food. However, the passage goes on to say that both food and the stomach are temporary and will eventually be destroyed by God because you will no longer be ruled by hunger or cravings of the flesh.

The second part of the passage is about the purpose of the body. It says that the body is not meant for sexual immorality, but for serving the Lord. This means that our bodies should be used in a way that honors God, rather than in a way that is sinful or immoral. The passage emphasizes that the Lord is meant to be the focus of our lives, rather than our physical desires or appetites.

When we marry, we bring honor to God (1 Corinthians 7:6-9)! Regarding premarital courtship, the man does the pursing before marriage, not the woman. According to Proverbs 18:22, the man should be looking for a wife and not a girlfriend. Then he will obtain a double-blessing or a good thing and have favor from the Lord.

Feminism, the modern version of the Eve motif, has single women chasing single and married men. Women must stop trying to trap men with their bodies. You might catch him, but anything trapped will eventually want to be free. Premarital sex is like drinking and driving because sexual intimacy can distort one's perception and you are unaware of danger until it is too late. There is a false sense of being in control when in reality, it is the exact opposite. There are hundreds of thousands of recordings of drivers under the influence, intoxicated because a person's sense of direction is distorted; thus, when people have premarital sex, their mentality, and focus are distorted, and the other person's feelings are uncertain. During premarital courtship, there should be no hugging or kissing, especially no sex! Each person's character is revealed during this time. Is the person's character holy or whorish?

A woman does not marry a man that she does not respect. The man has the power to make or break the marriage. The woman has the power to make or break the man. Let me make two closing comments to those of you who are single. Start living right now! Celebrate your singleness, whether temporary or permanent, and live a life of undivided devotion to the Lord. Live your life to the fullest for Jesus! Use your singleness to serve God. Single people with no children are not as distracted as much as those who are married with families. The world is passing away! In the final analysis, Jesus is the only one who can make and keep life sweet!

Scripture Reference:

1 Corinthians 7:6-9 (KJV) – "But I speak this with permission, and not of commandment. 7 For I would that all men were even as I myself. But every man hath his proper gift of God, one after this manner, and another after that. 8 I say therefore to the unmarried and widows, it is good for them if they abide even as I. 9 But if they cannot contain, let them marry: for it is better to marry than to burn."

Singleness is Not Loneliness

A few weeks ago, I was handed a note from one of the young women in our fellowship. She wanted to know when I would preach a sermon on singleness. I have preached at least three dozen such sermons, but I realize, this generation wants access at their fingertips. This manuscript is a response to this young lady's request. My target audience here is single women who have never married, without children, over the age of twenty-five. If you are 20-25, you must focus on getting your education and certifications, bachelors or post-graduate degrees, trainings, and career building. If you are a single mother and your child or children are over the age of 6, you must wait until that child, or those children are out of the home. Step-parenting is challenging, and there is the potential for additional problems to arise out of these types of relationships.

A single person is a person who is unwed, unique, whole, and complete. The Bible does not tell us something is wrong with being single. Unfortunately, some people seem as if being single is a curse or a punishment for having standards. But singleness is truly a blessing!

Be prepared to experience pressure from peer groups, family elders, cousins, siblings, and society at large to just give in to the first man that comes along. Some people feel pressure just because their friends are getting married. Parents can also add to that pressure from a meaningful place, but it can also be manipulative as well. Once upon a time I heard a single woman in exasperation proclaim, "I want to have children, but I have waited so long that my biological clock has become a gong!" Although this statement is funny, the hyperbolic nature of it strikes at the desperate longing some women feel. But men feel this longing too.

Men are single by choice, and women are single because the right man has not asked.

Even when you are married a child, sometimes, does not help matters. These pressures mount daily on those who are single. You must know how to handle them, or you will feel abandoned, become filled with self-loathing, or develop low self-confidence. Or you could even become depressed, swirling under tremendous anxiety and panic. Such pressures could even push you into making unwise decisions. Life can make you feel like a second-class citizen, a poster child for rejection and disappointment.

Pleasing God is the ultimate objective for all Christians, and there are no exceptions... single people. There are advantages to being single. Among them is that single persons can attend to the things of God without distractions. Loneliness is not peculiar to singles. It has to do with relationships. A person can be married and still be lonely. And a person can be single but not lonely. People become lonely when they are out of relationship with God and not honest with their accountability partner.

Finally, what should you do now? First, relax, and don't let your desires get out of hand. Do not become preoccupied with the thoughts of marriage and sex! Instead, enjoy this chapter in your life.

I'm Single, but I'm Not Stupid!

Dr. Laura Schlesinger, in her book, Ten Stupid Things Women Do to Mess Up Their Lives, wrote extensively of the ten areas she feels that women do stupid things when it comes to men. These areas are attachments, courtship, devotion, passion, cohabitation, expectations, conception, subjugation, helplessness, and forgiveness. This is a book that I recommend to ALL single women that come to me seeking advice about dating. I also use these writings to lead discussions with the singles group at my church. This labor of love is timeless and reaches the heart of women by causing a mind shift in how women see themselves in the eyes of a man.

The word stupid means marked by or resulting from unreasonable thinking or acting. Zig Ziglar called for a daily check up from the neck up to recognize "stinking thinking." The feminist would have you believe that men and women are the same. We are the same spiritually, see Galatians 3:28 "28 There is neither Jew nor Greek, there is neither slave nor free, there is neither male nor female; for you are all one in Christ Jesus." This passage is emphasizing the idea that all people are equal in the eyes of God and in the community of believers.

It states that there is no distinction between different groups of people, such as Jerusalem Jews or Jewish Greeks, war slaves or autonomous citizens, or men or women. Instead, all individuals are considered equal and united in their faith in Jesus Christ. This passage promotes the idea of inclusivity and equality within the Christian community. There are various perceptions, philosophies about life, systemic creeds, national identity, and political leanings that can be shared universally.

However, we are not the same sexually because men cannot have babies! In Genesis, God made Eve for Adam (Genesis 2:18-25). That difference made Adam exclaim, in Genesis 2:23, "and Adam said, this is now bone of my bones and flesh of my flesh; she shall be called woman." Generally, women are emotional first and physical second. Their emotional connection to the world is why words hurt women more than men.

Some women are driven by an intrinsic desire to become a mother. Please notice that

I wrote "some women" and not all women. Regardless, this yearning came after the fall in the Garden of Eden recorded in Genesis 3:16 "16 Unto the woman He said, "I will greatly multiply thy sorrow and thy conception. In sorrow thou shalt bring forth children; and thy desire shall be to thy husband, and he shall rule over thee." (See also Genesis 30:1; 1 Samuel 1:5-7). This is why women who deal with infertility have a much harder time coping and seek treatments to help with conception.

A woman's drive to be a wife and a mother can lead her to do some stupid things. This text shows us how this comes to pass in Isaiah 4:1 "And in that day seven women shall take hold of one man, saying, "We will eat our own food and wear our own apparel; Only let us be called by your name, to take away our reproach." This is a prophetic passage about the restoration of Jerusalem. The verse is often interpreted as a metaphorical representation of the desperation of women in a time of war or societal upheaval, where men are scarce, and women are left to fend for themselves. Here we see social anarchy – seven women to one man – where the women promise to support themselves, leading to reproach and disgrace. Who said it was a disgrace to be single? That is a lie from the very pit of hell.

There is social unrest, rampant homosexual pride, men choosing not to marry because the stats bear this out. But Colossians 2:10 states, "And ye are complete in Him, which is the head of principality and power." Women throughout the ages of time have felt deeply disgraced if they were unmarried and childless. We see this in the lament of Hannah. I Samuel 1-2:10 Hannah is a prominent figure in the Bible, specifically in the book of 1 Samuel. She was the wife of Elkanah and the mother of Samuel, one of the greatest prophets in Jewish history. Hannah was initially barren and deeply desired to have a child, so she prayed fervently to God for a son. God eventually granted her request, and she gave birth to Samuel, whom she dedicated to God's service.

There is also the instance of Rachel and her sister Leah. Rachel had no children with Jacob, but her sister Leah was consistently pregnant. She became so frustrated with her husband. Scripture records that in Genesis 30:1 "And when Rachel saw that she bore Jacob no children, Rachel envied her sister, and said unto Jacob, "Give me children, or else I die." Jacob redirected her to ask God.

Let us not fail to mention Elizabeth and Zacharias who were barren and in their old age. In Luke 1:5 -17 recounts the wonderful story of how the Creator of the Universe was preceded by his cousin, John the Baptist, to restore the people to repentance and back into covenant with Him as promised.

"Is nothing too hard for God?" is a phrase that comes from the book of Jeremiah 32:27. It is a statement that emphasizes the power and sovereignty of God and reminds believers that there is nothing too difficult or impossible for God to accomplish.

Mark 9:23 KJV: "Jesus said unto him, if thou canst believe, all things are possible to him that believeth." In the lesson of speaking with authority, Jesus awed his disciples and assured them that they will be able to do what He does and more when they are faithful to follow his example. In these instances, these women wanted children with their husbands. God had a plan for them, and He has a plan for you too.

Know that the years spent here are fleeting but God gives us comfort and relationship with Him. As singles desiring marriage, ask to the Lord to direct you to mentors of the same sex, operating in the fullness of their state of marriage or widowhood. Build a support system of like-minded singles at your local church. Focus on your needs so you can be an asset to countless future believers. Realize that what God has for you is for you. I will leave you with this scripture in Jeremiah 29:11 which says, "For I know the thoughts that I think toward you, saith the Lord, thoughts of peace, and not of evil, to give you an expected end." The Message Bible says "I know what I'm doing. I have it all planned out—plans to take care of you, not abandon you, plans to give you the future you hope for." The Contemporary English Version states "11 I will bless you with a future filled with hope— a future of success, not of suffering." That sounds like wedding vows to me!

Chapter 1 – I'm Single, So what!

Take a few moments in quiet reflection to form your "So What!" that will help shift your mindset in this area.

What is my focus scripture(s)?

_____

_____

_____

What did I learn?

_____

_____

_____

What does God want/expect from me?

_____

_____

_____

What will I choose?

_____

_____

_____

My "So What!" is:

_____

_____

Date:
_____

Letter to God

_____
_____
_____
_____
_____
_____
_____
_____
_____
_____
_____
_____
_____
_____
_____
_____
_____
_____
_____
_____
_____
_____

Personal Prayer Journal

Date:

Prayer Request:

Date Answered:

Praise & Thanksgiving:

Chapter 2
The Six Stages of a Relationship

I want to reiterate that I am coming from a biblical perspective in what I am about to say. I say this upfront because much of what is available in books and media comes from the view that men and women are on equal footing, and we are not! Please don't stop reading or throw my book into the trash can or into your donate pile. If you need to gather yourself, take a bath, take a long walk, or watch something on television.

Men and women can be similar intellectually, politically, socially, and spiritually. However, when it comes to relationships, it is different. In a relationship, God holds the man primarily responsible for the life of the relationship. This is why 90 percent of divorces are because of the man.

King Solomon says in Proverbs 18:22, "Whosoever finds a wife, finds a good thing, and obtains favor from the Lord." So very clearly, the man does the pursuing, not the woman. The man pursues, and the woman responds to the man's pursuit if she wants to. When a single woman seeks after a man, she puts the cart before the horse.

To understand this better, in this chapter I have outlined the stages of a healthy relationship. I will elaborate more on each stage in the following chapter.

1. The "Acquaintance Stage"

The word acquaintance means someone who knows someone slightly but is not a close friend. In life, we are always meeting new people. We meet people at the gym, grocery store, shopping, sporting events, family gatherings, and sometimes at Church, and these are people who, for the most part, will remain just an acquaintance and no more. You may have interests or hobbies in common. But the closeness or bond will not develop past a hello and how are you.

You probably will not remember their name or where you met. And when you run into each other it is like meeting for the first time all over again. However, they are not total strangers anymore. This is where many people get into trouble because they think that an acquaintance is a friend. It takes time to move from acquaintance to friendship. I will talk more about this in the section on Friendship.

You are still acquaintances with people that you find yourself spending more time with infrequently. These people have the potential to become more than friends. Your interaction is still that of surface level, someone you have discovered you have some places or maybe people in common, such as having the same employer but different location, attend the same church but serve in a different auxiliary, same university but different discipline of study, or may watch favorite sports at the same place but with different connecting friends. You would be interested in them, but nothing has been signaled or communicated. This stage should take about one to three years. Remember, my target audience is those who are single, never married, with no children. I am encouraging these guidelines to reach both men and women!

To have a great relationship takes time for it to develop. Therefore, time is not such a big deal, or at least it should not be a big deal. Rushing into a relationship within 2-3 weeks is a recipe for disaster and heartache! The divorce rate in America speaks for itself! When I examined the available data and the instances from my pastoral counseling background, most marital problems and divorces had a very short acquaintance period.

If there is interest, the acquaintance period will give you time to observe their motivations, work habits, character, mindset, and interests. You begin to formulate a picture of the person's life, and if the opportunity presents itself, ask yourself if you would be comfortable being a part of it and they a part of your life. Remember, you can take your time because you are not lonely and desperate. You are not looking for someone to rescue you from your world of singleness! Because there are so many benefits to being a single man or woman.

2. The "Brother/ Sister in Christ" Stage

The brother/ sister in Christ stage is the most critical stage by far. Because if a man and woman have not professed Christ as Lord, they do not possess the power to carry out the duties of marriage. This is especially true for men because, by nature, we are self-centered rascals. Like the commercial jingle, we want to "have it our way." Without the Spirit of God, a man and a woman will never experience what God had in mind for the institution of Marriage.

If the person you are interested in is not a Christian, you need to do what Forrest Gump's friend said to him, "Run, Forrest, Run!" Because if you stick around, you are asking for a lifetime of trouble. I'm not saying that an unsaved person would not make a good husband or wife, but I am saying not to take a chance with your life. The apostle Paul also gives a stern warning to the Church at Corinth in 2 Corinthians 6:14-18:

14 Be ye not unequally yoked together with unbelievers: for what fellowship hath righteousness with unrighteousness? And what communion hath light with darkness?

"Be ye not" in Hebrew and Greek means, do not do this! The saved man will love his wife as Christ loved the Church. Christ is our role model in marriage, and we cannot even try to live out our vows without loving Jesus Christ first. Thus, the Christian man, in all of his endeavors, will seek to please Christ in every area of his life.

The saved man's top priority in life is to please the Lord. His second priority would be to please his wife and he cannot do this if he is not a man after God's own heart. Remember that the marriage will last much longer than the courtship. Consequently, after marriage the man enters the phase of making sure he functions with his wife in harmony. Look at 1 Peter 3:7 which says, "Likewise, husbands, live with your wives in an understanding way, showing honor to the woman as the weaker vessel, since they are heirs with you of the grace of life, so that your prayers may not be hindered."

By nature, women know more about a man than men know about women because, with a man, everything is physical first and emotional second. Thus, we men are biologically driven by sleep, sex, food, sports, or food and sex. Women, on the other hand, are emotional first and physical second. Therefore, the average man has no clue about his wife's needs; therefore, he must exercise patience and become curious when he enrolls in the University of His Wife!

Finally, if the husband does not treat his wife right, his prayers will be thwarted. In 1 Peter 3:7 "...ye husbands, dwell with them according to knowledge, giving honor unto the wife, as unto the weaker vessel, and as being heirs together of the grace of life; that your prayers be not hindered." Every saved man knows the importance of prayer in his life. Prayer is how we communicate with our

God. It is one of the believer's primary defensive weapons against selfishness, sinfulness, and idolatry. When we pray, we depend upon God. The unsaved man cares nothing about the power and purpose of prayer. But to the believer, it is our lifeline!

Consequently, in this stage affection can emerge. In the Greek Philia (affectionate love) or friendship. Plato felt that physical attraction was not a necessary part of love, hence the use of the word platonic to mean, "without physical attraction.". In the life of the single saved man, he should pray and seek God's wisdom and direction before he tries to move the relationship to the next level. The unsaved man only pursues a woman for the sexual conquest. The saved man looks at her in the Spirit; because they are brother and sister in Christ, he will never intentionally disrespect her. Because, after all, she like a sister. in Christ. The Apostle Paul instructs Timothy in 1 Timothy 5:2, "The elder women, as mothers, the younger, as sisters, with all purity." Thus, there is a level of "Agape" love there for her first. It has markers of unconditional regard for their humanness.

3. The Friendship Stage

A friend is a person whom one knows and with whom one has a bond of mutual affection, typically exclusive of sexual or family relations. From this definition, notice it says, "Two people who have a bond of mutual affection"! In this stage, a man and a woman will begin spending more time talking on the phone and in person. They may share the same interests in a church ministry, have the same political views, or have opposing political views. The key is that they spend more time together and develop strong feelings for each other. This stage is vital and a great predictor of the success or failure of a marriage. To be a Christian friend can be an excellent asset for both people in their spiritual maturity.

In the friendship stage, there is also the opportunity for further discovery in the person's life. This stage is so great because there is no pressure to be one way or the other. Thus, a person can be themselves without all the pretenses. There is no auditioning. You get to be yourself and see the other person's true self. The Ancient Greeks call this kind of expression "ludus" as it a playful form of love. It describes the situation of having a crush and acting on it, or the affection between two young lovers.

This stage should last one to five years because there is no rush!

Finally, regarding the friendship stage, there cannot be any sexual activity. No formal hugs, no holding hands, no kissing in the mouth, and especially no sex. No oral sex, no mutual masturbation! No, no, no! I say this because for a man if he has sex outside of marriage with a woman, he loses respect for her. In the man's eyes, she is behaving like a loose woman with low self- respect! Sex outside of marriage is like drinking and driving; it affects your perception. In addition, the man won't trust her. Respect and trust are the two tracks of any healthy relationship, so "down tiger"! Remember, you are friends without benefits!

4. The Courtship Stage

It is at this stage that two essential moments take place. Dating one-on-one or exclusively and planning for Marriage. Notice I did not say planning for a wedding because there is a difference between a wedding and a marriage. In the next chapter, I will deal with weddings.

In this relationship stage, the man will let the young lady know he is interested in her and is more than just a friend. Before marriage, it's always the man's responsibility to take the relationship to the next level.

This can not be over stated. Look at the words of King Solomon in Proverbs 18:22, states, "Whoso finds a wife finds a good thing and obtains favor from the Lord."

Consequently, the man does the pursuing, not the woman. The man decides if he wants a woman. Remember, the woman responds to the man's advances. If she is not interested, she should let him know. Women, you are not selecting someone to go to the prom with you. You are beginning to choose a husband. So please, cut all the romance stuff out! This is serious business because selecting a mate will help determine your future and the future of your unborn children! Your selection will take you to the "Poor House" or to the "White House." This is why women need lots of prayers and godly counsel. Every Ruth needs a Naomi to help guide and instruct her on what to do, how, and when to do it. Let me repeat myself; you are not selecting a prom date; you are choosing your husband and the father of your children. This man will be your Prophet, Priest, Protector, and Provider of your family. So please do not play around at this stage.

Thus, in dating, both parties must be clear that they are in the mate selection process.

The man has indicated that he has prayed and sought the wisdom of his elders, and this is the woman God has placed in his Spirit. King Solomon says in Proverbs 11:14, "Where no counsel is, the people fall; but in the multitude of counselors there is safety." (KJV)

Therefore, it is a major decision for the man as well. He is selecting a woman to be his wife, the mother of his children. King Solomon also says in Proverbs 12:4, "A virtuous woman is a crown to her husband, but she that maketh ashamed is a rottenness in his bones" (KJV).

This is why both people must be saved and walk in the power of the Holy Spirit. Eros love to the ancient Greeks was considered to be super dangerous and very frightening as it involves a "loss of control" through the primal impulse to procreate. Eros is an intense form of love that arouses sexual feelings. At this point it becomes clear to both individuals that they are entering erotic territory. There must be agreement and understanding during this phase. With this foundation laid, let's look at dating and planning for marriage.

Dating is the time of profound discovery of the other person. Other than being saved, what do we have in common? What are our interests, favorite foods, and future or career plans? This is another reason why this is a radical time in the relationship. The time that is spent together is never alone late at night in one another's apartment or home alone. The woman, under no circumstances, should go to her his residence. Jesus says in Matthew 26:41, "Watch and pray, that ye enter not into temptation, the Spirit is willing, but the flesh is weak." (KJV)

I cannot emphasize enough that you do not play with the flesh. One of the sad comments I have heard is, "Pastor, we did not intend for it to go that far." But the damage can be hard to recover from. Because once you cross that bridge of sexual intimacy, you cannot behave like it never happened. If you cannot keep your hands off each other, you do what the Apostle Paul says in 1 Corinthians 7:9, "But if they cannot have self-control, let them marry, for it is better to marry than to burn." (KJV)

You do not get married just for the sex; you get married to bring glory to our God! The saved person understands and will obey. Abstinence also teaches sexual discipline in the man more than the woman. Women [43] generally are more disciplined in the sexual area than men. Men have the sexual drive, and women have the power of sex. Nothing will happen without her consent, and if something happens without her consent, it is rape! Most of the time, women will give sex to their boyfriend to keep them around.

Because today, dating, for the most part, is not for mate selection; it is for fun. However, some think they will get to know the person by dating. Therefore, dating must occur only within the context of courtship, so everyone knows where the relationship is going.

Secondly, within the courtship stage is the actual planning for the marriage. The difference between a marriage and a wedding is a one-time event that lasts no longer than 30-45 minutes maximum, and the exchange of vows takes less than ten minutes. However, marriage is until death do us part. This is why more prayer, preparation, and planning must be invested into the marriage. Most people will spend more time on college selection than on preparation for their marriage. The sooner they start marriage preparation training, the better. I suggest at least three to six premarital interviews. A thirty-day post-wedding discussion, followed by three, six, and nine-month check-ups. Because after marriage, there is a significant adjustment on the part of both the man and the woman.

The following information is what I call the four keys to a successful relationship. Notice I did not say perfect because there is no such thing as a perfect relationship. There are no perfect people. Therefore, I am unable to stress enough the vital importance of prayer, preparation, and planning. There are four keys to a successful relationship:

I. Jesus Christ must be number one in your life. This brings us back to the power of Jesus in the life of any relationship. The duties of both the man and the woman cannot be done without the power of the Holy Spirit (Colossians 1:18; Ephesians 5:22-33). For Christians, marriage is a ministry, and it is about pleasing our heavenly Father. The Apostle Peter says in 1 Peter 3:7 that if a man doesn't care for his wife, his prayers will be hindered. For a Christian man, the power of prayer in his life is essential. Thus, prayer is one of the primary weapons in Christian armor, and it is a must-have for his walk with God. Psalm 66:18 says, "If I regard iniquity in my heart, the Lord will not hear me."(KJV)

I cannot stress it enough that if you are involved with someone who is not saved, break it off now and run like the wind! The potential heartache and problems are not worth the tuxedo, wedding gown, cake, pictures, and food. Again, you are asking for problems because you directly violate the Word of God. Heed the warning in 2 Corinthians 6:14 "Do not be unequally yoked with unbelievers. For (A) what partnership has righteousness with lawlessness? Or (B) what fellowship has light with darkness?" (2 Corinthians 6:14-18). Women, this is especially true for you because your husband is to be the Prophet, Priest, Protector, and Provider of the home for his wife and children.

The unsaved person is spiritually incapable of being this to his wife and children. Please pay attention to the scripture 1 Corinthians 2:14-16, "14 The natural person does not accept the things of the Spirit of God, for they are folly to him, and who is not able to understand them because they are spiritually discerned. 15 The spiritual person judges all things, but is himself to be judged by no one. 16y "For who has understood the mind of the Lord so as to instruct him?" But we have the mind of Christ. (ESV) There is no accountability with an unsaved partner. You have no one to go and plead your situation to when he or she becomes overbearing, petulant, and/or a bully. Because God is not a partner in the marriage. (1 Corinthians 2:14-16).

II. Decide not to slide. The agreement is the power of life "3 Can two walk together, except they be agreed?" (Amos 3:3) ESV. There must be a written agreement. Habakkuk 2:2 says "Then the Lord answered me and said: "Write the vision And make it plain on tablets, That he may run who reads it." (NKJV) If it is not written down, it will soon become a forgotten conversation.

Once it is written down, it becomes a game plan for the success of your marital relationship. I would never enter a business arrangement without a written statement I could read and review. This is also true in a marriage agreement, there is a business side to your marital relationship, and it is excellent stewardship to do this.

It is also a way to hold yourself accountable and your mate responsible. For example, when watching football, unless it's the last two minutes of the half or the last two minutes of the game, they always huddle before the next play. This is to ensure everyone is on the same page and a successful outcome of the play. If there is any hesitation on the part of either person, that should send up a red flag!

With this being said, there are six crucial areas for a written agreement. I cover them more extensively in my book, *Marriage is Not for Children*. However, I will mention them here as well.

1. Finance. Approximately 85 percent of all divorces are because of money fights. The Bible says a lot about money and its usage. Jesus spoke more about money than He did about Heaven. A couple scriptures about money are Proverbs 22:7 which reads "The rich rules over the poor, And the borrower is servant to the lender." (NKJV) and Ecclesiastes 10:19 states' A feast is made for laughter, And wine makes merry; But money answers everything." (NKJV). Money also covers wills, life insurance, and retirement. I

am a huge Dave Ramsey fan because he shares biblical principles about debt-free. Mr. Ramsey also has a nine-week financial class called Financial Peace University.

Do your relationship a favor and take this course. It will be well worth your investment.

2. Intimacy. I will say much more about this in the final stage of Lovers. However, men and women see intimacy differently. The reason is that God made us with diverse needs and drives. However, before the wedding there can be no hugging, kissing, or holding hands...you get the picture!

3. In-laws. This is so crucial because in-laws can become outlaws. Read Genesis chapter 31 about Jacob and Laban. However, there are good accounts, such as the story of Ruth and Naomi.

4. Stepchildren. This can be a tricky situation if not managed with much prayer. The U.S. Census Bureau reports that there are 1300 new stepfamilies formed every day. The divorce rate is as high as 66 percent when "step-

parenting." My recommendation to single parents is that it is best to wait until those children finish high school and are out of the home before they marry or remarry. Don't sacrifice your children on the altar of your loneliness and lust.

5.   The Ex-factor. Because of the earlier statements about step-parenting, there needs to be much prayer put into a plan on how you will deal with your ex- or the children's biological parent. This subject also needs a lot of prayers and a written statement. I cover this subject in more detail in my first book about marriage.

6.   Religious Differences. I cannot stress enough how important it is not to marry someone from a different religious or theological background. For example, a Baptist should never marry a Catholic, and Methodists should never marry Mormons. And a Baptist should never marry a Jehovah's Witness. Do you get my drift?

III. The third area is to make it safe to connect. I have already covered this in stage three about being friends. Learn how to laugh together (Proverbs 17:22), have fun together, and have a hobby you can do together.

IV. The fourth and final area is to do your part. This means when you get married, you are about to change. I believe this is harder for us men because we are selfish. Thus, we must enter the University of Our Wives to learn more about them (1 Peter 3:7). Because of a woman's natural maternal instincts, she understands her husband better than he understands her. So, men, enroll now!

5. The Wedding Stage

This stage is where the woman takes over. Most women dream about being married and a mother when they are young. As a result, many young women have what is called a "hope chest." The hope chest, also called a dowry chest, cedar chest, trousseau chest, or glory box, is a piece of furniture traditionally used to collect items, such as clothing and household linen, by unmarried young women in anticipation of married life.

The wedding declares a man and a woman's intentions to be with each other for life. This ceremony can be public or private. But the primary intent is to declare their love for each other and enter this exclusive covenant. There can be many components of a wedding ceremony, but the most important is the exchange of vows between the man and the woman. The Bible is truly clear in stating that marriage is to be between a man and a woman as we see in 1 Corinthians 7:22 "Nevertheless, because of sexual immorality, let each man have his own wife, and let each woman have her own husband. God blesses no other arrangement. God does not recognize same sex marriages, nor does He sanction any form of polygamy! In Genesis chapter two, God created Eve for Adam, and that arrangement has never been changed!

When I am officiating a wedding, I always start my vows speaking to the man first because God holds the man primarily responsible for the life of the marriage (Proverbs 18:22). Normally, when a marriage dies, it is because the man has stopped "watering the grass" or the man has stopped courting and pursuing his wife. When performing a wedding, the next key component is the pronouncement by the Man of God. There is power in the pronouncement of a marriage, especially in the eyes of God. Regardless of what the couple had been doing before, but when the preacher pronounces them as husband and wife, it is no longer a sin in the eyes of God. Other elements could be added, such as a ring, an external indicator of internal commitment, a unity candle, etc. Still, again the two most important components are the vows between the man and woman and the pronouncement of them being husband and wife by the Man of God.

6. The Lover's Stage

This is the stage when physical and sexual contact is permissible and is permissible by God. Sex is a gift from God, for married couples only! It is not for those in a boyfriend and girlfriend relationship, nor is it for those who are not married. It is for a husband and his wife. God created sex for three reasons:

1.) Procreation, as said in Genesis 1:28. There has been only one virgin conception (Luke 1:34-37). 2.) Consummation of the marriage. Sexual intercourse is a sacred and special act between a husband and his wife. When a man's penis enters a woman's vagina, it creates a blood covenant, symbolizing the High Priest entering the Holy of Holies. This is when a husband and wife genuinely become one physically (cp. Genesis 2:24).

Divorce is exceedingly difficult because you are splitting people in half emotionally, spiritually, and sexually. This is why I believe non-marital sex is the kryptonite of a marriage. 3.) The third reason God created sex for marriage is for a husband and wife to express their love for each other. Sex is not only good for you, but it is good to you. The physical and psychological benefits of sex are immeasurable. The books of Proverbs and Song of Solomon have plenty to say about ecstasy and sexuality. One passage to reference regarding this is Proverbs 5:19, "Let her be as the loving hind and pleasant roe; let her breasts satisfy thee at all times; and be thou always ravished with her love."

As you can see, these actions are for married couples only. Sex is too powerful for the immature or amateur. Anne Ortlund, in her book, Up with Worship, compares the sexual act between a husband and wife to the worship of God. As stated in her book, "Just like in worship of God, we use our whole self – in other words, we give ourselves totally and completely to God. We hold nothing back. And when we finish worshiping our God, we feel so much intimacy with our God. Thus, the same way it is with our mate when we have sex, we hold nothing back. We share everything we have and everything we are during the time we are together. We are focused on our mate; their satisfaction is our only goal! Thus, when we have finished making that type of passionate love, we feel such closeness and warmth towards our mate".

Therefore, sexual acts are too precious and powerful to be played with outside of marriage's loving and committed covenant. Outside of marriage, this stunning act is so debasing and harmful. This is why in 1 Corinthians 7:9, the Apostle Paul states, "But if they cannot contain, let them marry: for it is better to marry than to burn."

Therefore, I say to you, as a Christian brother or sister, you can save yourself a lot of sorrow and regret by simply obeying the Word of God! The statistics are astronomical when couples are sexually active before they get married. About 95 percent of couples, I counsel have marital problems, are living together, or had premarital sex. The evidence does not lie.

Consequently, when violating the Word of God, you have unwanted pregnancies, which can lead to abortion. To me, this is America's second greatest sin; the first sin is slavery. Abortion brings a new reality for the woman who have to live with resentment and remorse over her choice for the rest of her life. Thank God for His grace because there is forgiveness. But women constantly tell me of the reminders and the sincere regret of their actions. Men have regrets, but I do not believe it is to the woman's level. This is simply because men do not carry the child in their bodies.

On average, researchers concluded that couples who lived together before marriage saw a 33 percent higher divorce rate than those who waited until they were married to live together. Part of the problem was that the cohabiters "slid into" marriage without much consideration. In this situation, I have found that, generally, the man will not respect or trust his wife. Because men are logical thinkers, they think that if a woman has sex with him and they are not married, then she will have sex with another man.

Most of the time, having sex with another man is the furthest thought from a woman's mind. Most wives that I know of get tired of having sex with their husbands and would not think of dragging another man into their life. For the most part, a woman is not made to have sex with more than one man.

Living together also increases the chances of domestic violence. When there is no respect or trust in a relationship, it can lead to domestic violence. When I was counseling a couple, a husband told his wife (during the session) that he "felt trapped." And anything that is trapped wants its freedom.

Finally, with all the information given, if you persist in engaging in premarital sex, I have only one thing to say. Either you are not saved and are very stupid, or you are both! My brothers and sisters, refrain from the sin of fornication; if you cannot, you should repent and get married as soon as possible. I advise those engaging in non-marital sex to stop it and repent of this sin or go ahead and get married! When you do it God's way, you will have His blessing in your life and the life of your marriage. Again, I admonish you to do it God's way and reap the blessings and benefits of God in your life. Not only for you but for your unborn children, think about them. They deserve a holy and happy home!

Women, non-marital sex will also increase your chances of being a single mother. One of the fastest-growing demographics today is single mothers. Over 37 million children are growing up in a single mother home. The sad reality is that most of these mothers were never married; they were abandoned by their boyfriends and left to fend for themselves.

Many of these mothers drop out of Church for various reasons, and these children are deprived of the blessing and benefits of attending Church. I was not a Christian in my younger years, but I thank the5L6ord daily for a Christian mother who took us to Church! My life was enriched, and I eventually got saved; the rest is history! Let me share these statistics and information with you.

Facts About Domestic Violence

- Most domestic violence incidents are never reported.

- Domestic/dating violence is a pattern of controlling behaviors that one partner uses to get power over the other person. It includes the act or threat of physical violence to gain control, emotional or mental abuse, and sexual abuse.

- 1 in 4 women will experience domestic violence during her lifetime.

- Women ages 20 to 24 are at the most significant risk of becoming victims of domestic violence.

- Domestic violence is the leading cause

of injury to women – more than car accidents, muggings, and rapes combined.

- Every 9 seconds in the U.S., a woman is assaulted or beaten.

- Every year, 1 in 3 women who are victims of homicides are murdered by her current or former partner.

Domestic Violence and the Impact on Children

- Every year more than 7 million children witness domestic violence in their homes.

- A Michigan study found that children exposed to domestic violence at home are more likely to systems of post-traumatic stress disorder, such as bed-wetting and nightmares, and are at greater risk than their peers of having allergies, asthma, gastrointestinal problems, headaches, and flu.

- Children who experience childhood trauma, including incidents of domestic violence, are at a greater risk of serious adult health problems, including tobacco use, substance abuse, obesity, cancer, heart disease, depression, and a higher risk for unintended pregnancy.

- Boys who witness domestic violence are twice as likely to abuse their own partners and children when they become adults.

- *(Futures Without Violence)*

Domestic Violence and Its Impact on Our Community

- According to the U.S. Department of Housing and Urban Development, domestic violence is the 3rd leading cause of homelessness among families.
- Survivors of domestic violence face high rates of depression or sleep disturbances, anxiety, flashbacks, and other emotional distress.
- Domestic violence contributes to poor health for many survivors. For example, chronic conditions like heart disease or gastrointestinal disorders can become more severe due to domestic violence.
- Domestic violence costs more than 37 billion a year in law enforcement involvement, legal work, medical and mental health treatment, and lost productivity at companies.

For more information, visit the National Domestic Violence Hotline website or contact an advocate by phone at 1-800-799-SAFE (7233), or 1-800-787-3224 (TTY).

More than just a bridge to safety, the National Domestic Violence Hotline is available to callers 24 hours a day, 365 days a year to provide services in more than 170 languages. Hotline advocates answer questions, provide safety planning and information, and directly connect callers to domestic violence resources available in their local calling area. All calls to the hotline are confidential and anonymous.

https://www.thehotline.org/

Advocates are available to help individuals who are Deaf and hard of hearing at 1-800-787-3224 (TTY) or by chat. They offer the same advocacy through chat services, available 24/7/365 for those affected by domestic abuse.

The hotline has partnered with the Abused Deaf Women's Advocacy Services (ADWAS) to ensure Deaf advocates are available to respond through email and video phone to those callers seeking help.

Website: https://www.adwas.org

Video phone (only for Deaf callers): 1-855-812-1001

Email: nationaldeafhotline@adwas.org

Chapter 2 – The Six Stages of a Relationship

Take a few moments in quiet reflection to form your "So What!" that will help shift your mindset in this area.

What is my focus scripture(s)?

_____

_____

_____

What did I learn?

_____

_____

_____

What does God want/expect from me?

_____

_____

_____

What will I choose?

_____

_____

_____

My "So What!" is:

_____

_____

Date:
_____

Letter to God

_____
_____
_____
_____
_____
_____
_____
_____
_____
_____
_____
_____
_____
_____
_____
_____
_____
_____
_____
_____
_____
_____

Personal Prayer Journal

Date:

Prayer Request:

Date Answered:

Praise & Thanksgiving:

Chapter 3
It's All About the Benjamins

I have laid the foundation of our study on stewardship and would like to share the steps of stewardship, which are:

1) Relationship with God through Jesus Christ (Ephesians 2:11-23).
2) Discipleship (Acts 2:42-42).
3) Worship (Psalms 100); and
4) Fellowship (1 Corinthians 11:1).

Stewardship is managing another person's property, finances, or household. As far as Christians are concerned, stewardship involves managing God's work through the Church. Evangelism. Kirk Nowery in his book, *The Stewardship of Life*, states "Everything that we have - every earthly resource - comes from a heavenly source". God is our faithful supplier, and His plan is that we become His faithful stewards (Psalms 24:1;118). Financial problems cause eighty-five percent of all divorces. Will Rogers said, "We spend money, we don't have to buy things we don't need to impress people we don't even like".

God wants us to do well. 3 John 2 says, "Beloved I wish above all things that thou mayest prosper and be in health, even as thy soul prospers." In the King James version of the Bible, there are 140 references to money, and ⅔ of Jesus's parables deal with finance.

There are two kinds of giving that I want to share, ordinary and extraordinary – in the sense of being regular and consistent. Extraordinary needs must be met with exceptional giving beyond all everyday commitments, such as our Burn the Note Campaign. Regular giving means being consistent. It includes tithes, which are the practice of giving a tenth of one's income or property as an offering to God.

Giving a tenth of your income or property extends into Hebrew history before the time of the Mosaic Law. The first instance recorded of tithing in the Bible occurs in Genesis 14:18-20, Genesis 28:22, and Malachi 3:8-10.

In the Old Testament, giving a tenth was to meet the material need of the Levite, the stranger, the fatherless, and the widow (Deuteronomy 26:12-13). The tithe was an expression of gratitude to God by His people. Basic to tithing was the acknowledgment of

God's ownership of everything in earth (Psalms 24:1).

In the New Testament, tithe and tithing appear only eight times (Matthew 23:23; Luke 11:42; 18:12 and Hebrews 7:5-6; 9).

All these passages refer to the Old Testament usage and current Jewish practice. Nowhere does the New Testament expressly command Christians to tithe. However, as believers, we are too generous in sharing our material possessions with the poor and for the support of Christian ministry. Christ Himself is our model in giving. Giving is to be voluntary – willing, cheerful, and presented in the light of our accountability to God (Matthew 6:19-21, 24, 2 Corinthians 9:7).

I want to encourage you to steward God's resources to the best of your ability. As I have previously stated, 85 percent of all divorces are due to arguments about money! Therefore, as a single person, I encourage you to take care of your finances. Many women get married for security, and I spell security m-o-n-e-y. If you are financially stable, you can make a better mate selection.

According to the Word of God, men are to care for their wives and children. The Apostle

Paul says in 1 Timothy 5:8, "But if any provide not for his own, and especially for those of his own house, he hath denied the faith, and is worse than an infidel."

If you plan to get married, you must, as a Christian man, have your financial house in order. Your stewardship is a witness to your perspective mate, and the world. Spend money wisely and invest well. In the King James Version of the Bible, there are 140 references to money, and two-thirds of Jesus' parables deal with finances. You must know and understand that one of Satan's ways of defeating us is in the area of finances. So, set your financial house in order.

There are some simple things I suggest:

1) Pay your Tithes. In Matthew 23:23, Jesus never said for us to stop tithing. A tithe is 10 percent of your income. Giving a tenth of your income or property extends into Hebrew history before the time of the Mosaic Law. The first instance recorded of tithing in the Bible occurs in Genesis 14:18-20, Genesis 28:22, and Malachi 3:8-10. The tithe is an expression of gratitude to God for His blessing. Basic to tithing was the acknowledgment of God's

ownership of everything on the earth (Psalm 24:1).

2) Pay yourself. You should be saving about 8 percent or more of your income.

3) Establish an Emergency Fund. You should have at least three to six months of emergency savings. Consequently, you will not have to panic if you lose your job.

4) Get a Will and a Living Trust.

5) Take Dave Ramsey's Financial Peace University and get out of debt! Get rid of all your debts (Luke 7:41-50), including credit cards. If you have obligations, pay them, and pay them on time (Romans 13:8). It is a poor testimony for a Christian not to pay their bills. I strongly encourage all singles to take this class. You will not regret it, I promise you! Just go online to www.daveramsey.com. There are always Financial Peace courses available.

<u>Scripture Reference:</u>

Ecclesiastes 10:19 (KJV) - A feast is made for laughter, and wine maketh merry: but money answereth all things.

Once you have conquered your fear, you can face the reality of the difference between loneliness and being alone. There are so many lonely married people that the term "married single" was coined. This means a person is usually married, usually, a woman who lives as a single person. Her husband rarely does anything with her or takes her anywhere.

Alone, yet not lonely, you have many opportunities to help someone else and be involved in the Kingdom of God. So, fill up that time helping others who need your help because so many ministries could use your gifts and talents.

I have included more Prayer Journal pages in the back of this book so that you can begin communicating your prayers to God. I want you to write down your prayer requests, enter the date of the request, and when God answered your prayers, bless and thank Him because He WILL answer!

Chapter 3 – It's All About the Benjamins

Take a few moments in quiet reflection to form your "So What!" that will help shift your mindset in this area.

What is my focus scripture(s)?

_____

_____

What did I learn?

_____

_____

_____

What does God want/expect from me?

_____

_____

_____

What will I choose?

_____

_____

_____

My "So What!" is:

_____

_____

Date:
_____

Letter to God

_____
_____
_____
_____
_____
_____
_____
_____
_____
_____
_____
_____
_____
_____
_____
_____
_____
_____
_____
_____
_____
_____
_____
_____

Personal Prayer Journal

Date:

Prayer Request:

Date Answered:

Praise & Thanksgiving:

Chapter 4
The Protocol, The Promise and The Peace

There is nothing like being spiritually conscientious. This leads to mental, financial, physical, and emotional awareness because of your foundational relationship. The King of the Universe, the Keeper of Promises, and the God of Peace is already in love with you. He keeps courting you with every blessing, every new day, every chance to begin again. His plans for us are amazing yet conditional.

Just like every relationship we are in planning, thinking, choices, and actions must be made. These actions are intentional and affect our present, future, and eternity. As the adage goes, "God don't bless no mess!" If every aspect of your life is not surrendered and submitted to God, it leaves room for a lackadaisical attitude and marginalizes what He expects and what you eventually do. Men are exposed to the Manosphere sector of the internet of male influencers that degrade women, In-cels (involuntarily celibate males), Red Pill-ers (affirm manhood/fatherhood and desire a household with traditional values, i.e., mother home, homeschool, self-sufficient, etc.,), Mgtow-ers (men going their own way), and male feminists (men who champion the economic and political equality of the sexes) propelling their poison into the ethos. It will be difficult for faithful women who desire marriage and motherhood to attract men who have biblical standards.

I want you to know and realize that the man that God will covenant you with will be a man that will live for Him and die for you. This man will lead from a place of respect because he is submitting to the authority of Jesus Christ. He will be sensitive to the leadership of the Holy Spirit and emotionally ready to minister to your needs as his wife.

Sounds idealistic? Maybe, but from the standpoint of the 18.5 million fatherless children in this country, there is a dire need for men who love God and desire a family. It is imperative for women who love the Lord and live a lifestyle of holiness to be preparing themselves for their future spouse. They must acquire skills that lead to a balanced and harmonious home life. More than 85.4 million singles have never married in this country, and 60 percent are men. So, the call to single, Christian, and unattached women to get ready is hopeful and sincere, not dire or depressing. Move from a scarcity mindset to abundance because in Christ, God's promise to do exceedingly and abundantly above all that we could ask or think" is true when we obey him; it is just as true for you even in your singleness.

If it is not clear, women are the only individuals that can conceive and gestate a child inside their bodies, in their womb. It matters not that learned people and doctors want to remain politically correct about the definitions, genders, and sexes. Scripture tells us that God created them male and female.

Also, misogynistic rhetoric and feminist ideology do not have a biblical context. The New Testament scripture tells us that God does not regard one person above another. The LGBTQIA2SP+ (pedophilia, hebephilia, polyamory, pansexual, polygamy, bestiality, kink) agenda that has invaded our public spaces and schools is to undermine the authority of the parents. This creates a generation of confused, godless, and suicidal young adults.

These concepts and others have solidly derailed the proper relationships between men and women. They are a total deception from the enemy of our souls to divide and keep nuclear families from being formed and then multiplying. If you have not yielded these concepts into the light of scripture by recognizing them as spiritual bondage, making culture your god and right think your guide, then as we move forward in this chapter will not connect with you.

Yes, being single is a beautiful privilege, especially when you have intentionally chosen the right people and time to get yourself ready.

As believers, we have careers to nurture, education to obtain, and ministries to serve the Kingdom of God here on earth. But it would help if you remembered that you could not serve others from an empty cup... keep it full. Serve from the overflow of your cup.

Knowing your purpose in life is vital to stabilizing your identity in Jesus Christ and as a person. Being single is not an identity; it is a lifestyle. It is not a hall pass to have sex with as many people as possible and then settle down. Singlehood is a phase of life; for some, this phase is short, yet it will be lifelong for others. Just remember you are already in a relationship with the lover of your soul.

People meet in all types of places, and there is an attraction but not all lead to connection. Please be mindful and wise when meeting strangers, spending time with people you do not know well, and becoming hopeful with each new connections. There is a danger and a danger of disappointment that can deplete your optimism, wreck your peace of mind, leading you to compromise your body. Scripture tells us. This means that we are joined with God by marriage and lordship spiritually. When we sin, as a bride and a member of the body of Christ, fellowship is broken not amputated. Sexual sin is spiritual and physical. The other sins are projected outward like gossiping, lying, and slander the tongue expelling sound. When there is stealing we see it, take it by our hands, or gain possession by breaking the law of covetousness. Same with murder which hands or another object or toxic mode with planning starts in the mind then leads to the premeditated act.

But the Holy Spirit resides in the temple not made by hands. The act of sex, touching, penetrating, exchange of fluids, can be done in secret but God knows. He bought us with a precious price and we are commanded to flee fornication and then honor God in our soul and bodies. We are not permitted to prostitute ourselves or alienate ourselves from God's presence.

Dating is another pitfall the resistance uses to get us off the path of holiness by turning loneliness into sin and the weekend into a prison. Just because a man has sex with a woman does not mean he wants to marry that woman. No amount of orgasm or sexual pleasure is going to change this knowledge. The sad realization is that many women believe that if a man enters their body, he will let the woman enter his heart. This is never the case. There is a point when you must confront the reality of the power that God has given you, not only in Him as a believer but the tremendous power and responsibility of selecting a mate for marriage. You hold potent sexual energies that are God-given. So rest in your femininity. You have no rival in this area.

The transgender agenda will never succeed when you, as a woman, do not give up this area to the enemy that seeks to usurp your rightful place. You must push back on this or risk competing with transgendered males for male attention. There is beauty, softness, and the ability to comfort in your presence. You do not lose anything being a woman, but you gain freedom from distorted messages when you lean into your femininity. Trying to fit in with the world, making yourself small, or being perceived as a none threat to a man's masculinity are not biblical concepts. But be advised that with power comes responsibility, and God holds you responsible, sexually pre-marriage because of your potential to carry life in your body.

If this is an area in your life that you have yet to surrender to the Lord, I implore you to position your lifestyle to regard sex only for marriage. Scripture tells us that the marriage bed is undefiled. This means that in this union, God blesses sexual creativity, sexual expression, and sexual release. With agreement, whatever happens between these two people, in their bedroom and home, does not have to be dignified or justified to other people, the church, or the government.

Outside these parameters, the believer is wide open to demonic oppression, soul ties, condemnation, abuse (financial, physical, emotional, and verbal), catfishing, stalking, unwed pregnancy, sexually transmitted disease, scamming, shame, and many other consequences. None of these things are the fruits of the spirit. Choose to be wholly God's until he presents you whole and complete to your wedded spouse. You are promised the peace of God as scripture says in I Corinthians 9:27 "But I discipline my body and keep it under control, lest after preaching to others I myself should be disqualified." and fleeing fornication.

You are single, which means you are not married. Your lifestyle is one of an individual's. You can be single but in college, single but living with your parents or other relatives, single but living with roommates, or single but have lived with your boyfriend(s) in your past before you surrendered your life to Jesus Christ. Allow space and time for God to help renew your mind about your singleness as a lifestyle that affirms your worth as a woman, a believer, and a person ready for a committed relationship.

It takes a while to get to know someone, especially in intimacy, compatibility, and expectations. Boundaries are the key to setting up solid connections with another person. Inside these boundaries, a world of wonder is still worth exploring inside you. Past relationships, past sexual partners, past betrayals, past disappointments, past failures, past sexual assaults and molestations, past careers, and past experiences of racism, inequality, and injustice could hold ramifications in connecting with the opposite sex in the future and with your desire to mate. While you wait for the Lord to bring you together with your partner and potential ministry mate, you can take action to bring God's fullness into your life on earth as it is in heaven.

The protocol is the same for every believer, but your emphasis will be on holiness. Cast all your sexual desire and frenetic energy at the foot of the cross. Allow the blood of Jesus to cover and bless you, giving you favor with Him and the person you are to bond with and marry.

The waiting takes on the concept from Isaiah 40:31 "31 But they that wait upon the Lord shall renew their strength; they shall mount up with wings as eagles; they shall run, and not be weary; and they shall walk, and not faint." (KJV). The central relationship that we have is our relationship with God. We relate to He through a consecrated life of prayer. This is not where God is reduced to being a fairy godmother or a sugar daddy. Lord- gimme sessions have no place in the life of a mature believer. The true meaning of prayer is intercession for other people and their situations, mentioned and unmentioned. We pray for people in our sphere of influence, conditions that affect the less fortunate. We pray for people in leadership, our families, our places of worship, our jobs, and our city, state, and national leadership. We pray that God's will be done here on earth as in heaven.

When the Lord prompts you, pray for your future spouse and their family. You will continue to have to do this even once you are engaged and married. Your family-in-law will have to be on your prayer list for obvious reasons. I hope that they become your family-in-love because of the love you will genuinely develop with each other as husband and wife.

Meditation will have to be another aspect of maintaining focus on the Lord. This process is a meditation on scripture. Many cell phone apps, websites, and YouTube channels can assist you with this process. The scripture says to meditate on the word day and night. You must surround your mind and space with music and scripture affirming your commitment to living for God. There is no reason to spin in a cycle of sadness when God is there and loving on you. It is His spirit that is sustaining you and keeping you balanced. When you deny God access spiritually, your emotions are susceptible to mental attacks.

The mind begins to make statements against what God says about you in scripture. The scriptures Psalm 139:14 "I will praise You, for [a]I am fearfully and wonderfully made; Marvelous are Your works, And that my soul knows very well." (NKJV) and Luke 12:7 "But the very hairs of your head are all numbered. Do not fear therefore; you are of more value than many sparrows." and Zepahniah 3:17 "The Lord your God in your midst, The Mighty One, will save; He will rejoice over you with gladness, He will quiet you with His love, He will rejoice over you with singing." (NKJV) wonderfully made called you from your mother's womb by name, know the hairs on your head twirl around excitedly over you."

Just know that you do not have to wait to go to hell to experience torment   because the torment in your mind is intense. That is why keeping your mind on Jesus is essential to keep faithfulness and not settle or compromise on the promises of God.

Having and expressing gratitude to the Lord is consequential to a life set apart for holiness. We can skyrocket to the next level with God just by being grateful to Him for just being God and God alone. In the believer's life, we express ourselves to the lover of our souls through worship and praise. Every living person and all the living things, this includes animals of all kinds, plants, flowers, trees, the waters teeming with life, fowls, and everything that flies or crawls, are commanded to praise the Lord (Psalm 138:4; Romans 15:11). You can praise the Lord with singing (Isaiah 12:5; Psalm 9:11), with projecting your voice out loud (Psalm 33:1; 98:4), with the movement of the body (Psalm 150:4), and with various instruments playing melodies (1 Chronicles 13:8; Psalm 108:2; 150:3-5).

These can be replete hymns or original compositions of scripture, psalms, hymns, and spiritual songs.

Capture your gratitude for the Lord by buying or creating a Gratitude Journal. There are many online templates, and many retail stores sell different types of journals. Or you can take a regular composition notebook, decorate it, date it, and list how God showed up for you that day. Or you can start your day with a gratitude list of three to five entries.

Praise is joyful and is intricately connected to thanksgiving as we offer back to God. Even in a marriage relationship, you must show appreciation to your spouse. Learn to appreciate God in your singlehood. Bless him for how he provides and shows up mightily in your life. Praise is the breath's oxygen permeating our relationships with God and others. You can praise your family members, friends, or boss that extend kindness and favor. This action does not require anything of you, just a grateful heart.

When you show this type of gratitude, you are truthfully acknowledging the righteous acts of another. God is worthy of praise; He is just so wonderful in keeping his promises and keeping us from hurt, harm, and danger. In Psalms we read 18:3 "3 I will call upon the Lord, who is worthy to be praised: so shall I be saved from mine enemies." (KJV)

Another form of praise denotes a type labeled "sacrifice of praise." Usually, a heart that has been humbled and purified by fire, choosing to honor God despite the chaos and pain one is experiencing. There are times when God does not change outcomes. Life unfolds in opposite ways than what is desired. Psalm 51:16-17 reads, "You do not delight in sacrifice, or I would bring it; you do not take pleasure in burnt offerings. My sacrifice, O God, is a broken spirit; a broken and contrite heart you, God, will not despise."

When one feels this level of despair, injustice, or disappointment, the last thing one wants to do is bring that pain before the Lord. But I challenge you to let that be the first thing you do, to bring your woes, pain, and primal groaning to God. Even though the situation of singleness feels hopeless and bleak with little to no options for meeting single Christian people, still praise Him.

We do not have to understand why this mindfulness is necessary, but it brings us to a place of acceptance and understanding that God's will, will be done on earth as it is in heaven. God will never fail and is working all things together for the good of them called unto His purpose. Coming to God through tears and pain is intentional because in doing so, we acknowledge that God is still God, and Hebrews 13:5 states "Let your conduct be without covetousness; be content with such things as you have. For He Himself has said,

"I will never leave you nor forsake you."
(NKJV). His Word states in Nahum 1:7 "The
Lord is good, a refuge in times of trouble.

He cares for those who trust in him,"
(NKJV) Command your will to shout and sing
His praises like in Psalm 135. The more you
exercise your will to come to the Lord first,
He is honored, and our faithfulness to Him
grows deeper, stronger, and unshakeable.

In Hebrews 13:15, we are commanded to
"Therefore by Him let us continually offer the
sacrifice of praise to God, that is, the fruit of
our lips, [a]giving thanks to His name."
(NKJV). We do not praise or withhold credit
from God based on whether he does our
bidding or made someone choose us. What
God does for us is evident because he is our
first and only love. Until God brings you
together with the spouse ordained for you,
He is your sole focus and your only source.
The only true and living God worthy of praise
which can only flow continually from a
worshiping heart in good times and bad.

Praise is usually labeled as loud but
joyful, marked by uninhibited movement and
clapping. Worship, however, has different
manifestations. We read verses like,
"Worship the Lord in the beauty of holiness";

(Psalm 96:9)." And "Come let us worship and bow down." (Psalm 95:6). Often, worship is coupled with the act of bowing or kneeling, which shows humility and repentance. Through true worship, we invite the Holy Spirit to speak to, convict, and comfort us. Through worship, we realign our priorities with God and acknowledge Him once more as the rightful Lord of our lives. Praise is linked with thanksgiving; worship is bound to the actions of surrendering. It is impossible to worship God plus any other source Luke 4:8b reads "For it is written, 'You shall worship the Lord your God, and Him only you shall serve.'" (NKJV). When you are in a state of worship, your posture is humble. Usually, during worship, you may find yourself weeping, bowed, on your knees, and or with your arms and hands raised. During your time of worship, you might begin with praise and then transition into this type of physical expression. God requires a heart that truly seeks Him, and He desires and deserves pure, holy, and uninhibited praise and worship. In the Bible, the book of Psalms is a large body of songs that can be spoken, sung, and used for meditation.

After moving through the protocol, we abide in God's peace regardless of what we see and how we feel. This is a daily, hourly, moment-to-moment mindful choosing to stay firmly planted like a tree planted by the waters of God's word, His will. God is still on His throne, ordering our steps and working in our lives for His glory and our good. The Lord's peace abides when we walk daily in a constant mindset of prayer, meditation, and gratitude. The fantastic clarity that comes with this harmony extends to the body and the mind.

Honestly, examine yourself from a physical standpoint. Look at yourself in a full-body mirror and take time to understand that you are beautiful and unique. Create a list of areas you need and would like to invest in. Take your time with this process. When something comes up to your awareness, recognize it by writing it down in your journal or on the paper where you track this awareness.

Frequently, take a few moments each month to spend time with your mirror, your calendar, and your budget. You may be asking yourself, why do these things? Using a mirror for reflecting cannot be spiritual. But be assured that you want to assess your visible self, not from a place of vanity. Touch your skin to check for dryness, and behold subtle changes, lumps, or protrusions. This is much different than being critical of yourself to compare yourself to other people physically. To avoid your mirror is not godly, nor does it show gratitude to the God that created you. You must be in touch with your body, appreciating every curve, how you look when you are happy, how you hold your body, and how you carry your weight.

Know the attractive parts of your features and accentuate these attributes. If the Holy Spirit is leading you to grow to the next level that produces and shapes the best confidence and healthy self-regard, take the time to self-assess. Other people can see you, even when you are not looking. Fix what needs to be fixed. Is it your teeth? Make a dentist appointment, or do you need to stop your hair from breaking due to stress or the wrong shampoo? See a beautician! Do you need to remove clothes that are too revealing or no longer fit? See a stylist to know what colors and clothes flatter your body type. Do you bite your nails, or do you like to walk around barefoot? Start going to the nail salon and find a good nail tech.

Are you feeling run down and out of breath more, or have you noticed a loss of stamina, needing to drink more coffee during the day? Get a medical checkup and set appointments for your annual physical. Seek optimal health and longevity by eating well-balanced meals, taking vitamins, nutrients, and supplements. Giving this attention to yourself is an investment of time and money. But being consistent will pay off and bring contentment to your home and total personal stability, whether single or married. You can remain soft and feminine, knowing that everything you get into your life is for the glory of God.

Your sensuality is not the same as your sexuality. The former is a mode and mood of being, including activating the senses and enhancing sight, taste, sound, smell, and touch. There is physical pleasure in the body's movements, but sensuality does not require anyone else to participate. Sexuality is the physical, uninhibited expression of your attraction preference, amplifying your sense of worth. Your ideas of love and the act of loving become displayed during this set-apart time. When you are expressing and sharing yourself this way, it must be within the confines of marriage. Without this covenant, your self- esteem, body image, and mental health are harmed, placing you under heavy conviction and potentially life-long consequences.

As you begin to grow in the Lord and expound on being a good steward of your body and resources, you may discover areas that you may need to address from a family of origin, boundary setting, depression, or trauma-related issues. When you recognize a need for counseling, seek pastoral sessions, or you can be referred to Christian counseling. While you are single is the time to address these issues that may arise for you. Some things from the past must be processed through therapy and then placed at the foot of the cross to be covered by the blood of Jesus so you can be complete and whole.

The beauty the Lord sees in you will not be lost on the person he has set aside just for you. Your wellness will be from the inside to the outside. Resting well is vital to your overall mental and physical well-being. Knowing your body and how much sleep you need is essential. This is how you can measure your stamina during the day. If your sleep has become interrupted due to stress, overthinking, ruminations, or health changes, this must be addressed as soon as possible.

There are over-the-counter sleeping aids that are none habit-forming that can be taken occasionally. Assess your sleep hygiene next to see if you are exacerbating your restlessness and fatigue. Check for room temperature, smells, ambient sounds, light, and screens and adjust accordingly. You can also use a prescription from the doctor; use it as directed, being aware of the side effects.

Reading scripture before bed or listening to scripture as you sleep is a helpful aid to resting. You can set a sleep timer on your device so it will go off without disturbing your sleep cycle. Be careful with the types of teachers you listen to and podcasts that entertain you. What messages are being pushed by these influencers? Even if they are Christian, some have become influenced by worldly ideology. They desire fame, influence, and wealth by doing and saying anything for clout and to go viral. This could lead to the authority of Christ being compromised. But these people will reap what they have sown. God will always triumph! Stay faithful to scripture and your local church ministries.

By spending time with your money, you can budget effectively and tithe correctly. You will know how and where your money is going. As a believer, buying luxury labels and goods is fine, but not if you are not paying your bills. If your credit score needs repair while you are single is time to address your spending and saving habits. Knowing how to invest money, create passive income, or start your own business increases your awareness of the market and could be attractive to your potential spouse.

This is equally yoked if this person is obtaining the same financial literacy. Improving your credit score, staying out of debt, and paying your bills on time are attractive to a possible partner in marriage. Do you need to attend school to begin, continue, or complete your education? Are you in your career, but you feel stuck? Do you feel like it is time to start your own business? Do you feel called to go into ministry? While you are single it is the time to invest in yourself and take chances.

Time goes by so fast, but by keeping a calendar, you can log how you spend your time and keep up with due dates for projects, bills, and appointments. This helps you stay trustworthy and keep your word. Your potential mate needs to know that you are dependable and not a dependent.

It takes two whole and complete people choosing to love God and serve each other to have a healthy union. Your habits, good or bad, can become a source of conflict and reveal incompatibility early in the relationship. Stay accountable to godly women in your real life, and know what God expects from you as a single woman who wants to become married to His choice for you.

The promise comes from Psalm 37:4, which reads "Delight yourself also in the Lord, And He shall give you the desires of your heart." (NKJV) If you focus on pleasing God in all areas of your life, even submitting those areas of uncertainty, He does the giving. Prayer pleases God. Tithing pleases Him as well. Caring for your body and mind pleases God. Celebrating His goodness and mighty deeds pleases Him too.

If you do not know yourself, have not spent time loving Him, or have not accomplished the basics in life, how will you know your desires? He knows you want or do not want marriage, but most importantly, he knows when to give and protect you. As a woman of God, you will attract different types of men. The key is to know yourself so that you can select God's best for you.

Chapter 4 – The Protocol, Promise, and Peace

Take a few moments in quiet reflection to form your "So What!" that will help shift your mindset in this area.

What is my focus scripture(s)?

_____

_____

_____

What did I learn?

_____

_____

_____

What does God want/expect from me?

_____

_____

_____

What will I choose?

_____

_____

_____

My "So What!" is:

_____

_____

Date:

_____

Letter to God

_____

_____

_____

_____

_____

_____

_____

_____

_____

_____

_____

_____

_____

_____

_____

_____

_____

_____

_____

_____

_____

Personal Prayer Journal

Date:

Prayer Request:

Date Answered:

Praise & Thanksgiving:

Chapter 5
Frequently Asked Questions

1. What boundaries should I have when dating someone?

There should be no physical contact of any kind when dating. This includes holding hands, kissing, and especially hugging. Also, you should not spend any time alone with each other because this can lead to satisfying self-desires, sin and ultimately allowing Satan access to the relationship.

2. What should I do if I have premarital sex with my partner?

You should get married immediately or end the relationship immediately!

3. What common mistakes do most people make in relationships?

One of the most common mistakes is becoming involved with a non-Christian. The Bible clearly states believers should not be involved with unbelievers (2 Corinthians 6:14-18). You can save yourself a lot of heartache and trouble by obeying God!

4. How can I be content as a single person?

You can be content by not focusing on your singleness. Instead, you should focus on your walk with the Lord. As a single person, you can do more for the Kingdom of God because Marriage has a lot of distractions (cp. 1 Corinthians 7:32-35).

5. Can single men and women be friends?

There is always a possibility, especially once you reach your twenties, because God made man and woman for each other. And it is tough, if not impossible, to keep a platonic relationship. Many have tried, and many have failed. I would advise not to try it because, most of the time, someone will get hurt. Your emotions can be hazardous, so do not even attempt to do it. The more time you spend with someone, the more you get attached to that person, and the harder it is to let go if one person wants out.

6. Should a woman take the initiative with a man in pursuing a romantic relationship with him?

NO, NO, NO! Proverbs 18:22 clearly states that the man does the pursuing, not the woman. The idea of a woman pursuing a man is rooted in radical feminism. Therefore, radical feminism is totally against the Word of God. In Genesis, God created Adam and Eve,

104

and again I repeat, the man does the pursuing and not the woman. By this, a woman will know that the man wants her to be his wife, not a "friend with benefits." The man should initiate, and the woman should respond if she is interested. Remember, a man _will_ have sex with you, but it does not mean he wants to marry and care for you until "death do you part." Again, for the 100th time, women should stay in their place and let the man pursue them! Once you are married, you can run your husband worldwide and have sex with him as often as you want because he is your husband!

7. What does a healthy friendship look like with a man/ woman?

Again, let me reiterate that a man and woman who are unrelated and attracted to each other can never have a platonic relationship. God created Eve for Adam. Some men and women are drawn to each other naturally and sexually by God. Therefore, you must be crystal clear about the purpose of this relationship so that no one's feelings will be hurt. You should ask yourself, "Are we just friends, or is something else expected"? You must be open and honest from the start because Friendship is the basis of a great relationship.

8. What are biblically based dating practices that I can use when dating?

Dating in the Bible was always for mate selection and never just for pleasure, like it has been in America since World War II. The concept of dating began at the turn of the 20th century. Prior to the late 1900s, courtship was much more private, unemotional affair. A young man and a young lady were always chaperoned by an adult, usually by their parents. With the invention of the automobile, a young man and a young woman could go off and be alone, which was not a promising idea. Because now anything can happen when a young man and a young woman are alone!

9. How can I develop godly friendships with single and married brothers and sisters in Christ?

Instead of developing friendships, concentrate on fellowshipping with other brothers and sisters in Christ. Then as you worship and fellowship together, the Spirit of God will lead you into developing special friendships that will last for years.

10. As an older Christian single, how do I manage the fear of being alone?

First, as believers, we do not live in fear. The Apostle Paul states in 2 Timothy 1:7, "For the Spirit God gave us does not make us timid, but gives us power, love, and self-discipline." Also, see 1 John 4:15 and Job 3:25.

Chapter 5 – Frequently Asked Questions

Take a few moments in quiet reflection to form your "So What!" that will help shift your mindset in this area.

What is my focus scripture(s)?

_____

_____

_____

What did I learn?

_____

_____

_____

What does God want/expect from me?

_____

_____

_____

What will I choose?

_____

_____

_____

My "So What!" is:

_____

_____

Date:
_____

Letter to God

_____
_____
_____
_____
_____
_____
_____
_____
_____
_____
_____
_____
_____
_____
_____
_____
_____
_____
_____
_____
_____
_____
_____

Personal Prayer Journal

Date:

Prayer Request:

Date Answered:

Praise & Thanksgiving:

Personal Prayer Journal Pages

Personal Prayer Journal

Date:

Prayer Request:

Date Answered:

Praise & Thanksgiving:

Personal Prayer Journal

Date:

Prayer Request:

Date Answered:

Praise & Thanksgiving:

Personal Prayer Journal

Date:

Prayer Request:

Date Answered:

Praise & Thanksgiving:

Personal Prayer Journal

Date:

Prayer Request:

Date Answered:

Praise & Thanksgiving:

Personal Prayer Journal

Date:

Prayer Request:

Date Answered:

Praise & Thanksgiving:

Personal Prayer Journal

Date:

Prayer Request:

Date Answered:

Praise & Thanksgiving:

Personal Prayer Journal

Date:

Prayer Request:

Date Answered:

Praise & Thanksgiving:

Personal Prayer Journal

Date:

Prayer Request:

Date Answered:

Praise & Thanksgiving:

Personal Prayer Journal

Date:

Prayer Request:

Date Answered:

Praise & Thanksgiving:

Personal Prayer Journal

Date:

Prayer Request:

Date Answered:

Praise & Thanksgiving:

Personal Prayer Journal

Date:

Prayer Request:

Date Answered:

Praise & Thanksgiving:

About the Author

Dr. B.W. McClendon, Sr.'s magnetic personality, blended with an explosive sermon and expository speaking style, has drawn audiences nationwide for over five decades. As a result, he has emerged as one of this generation's most influential spiritual leaders. As Senior Pastor of the St. James Missionary Baptist Church in Austin, Texas, his priority is expansion through evangelism.

Dr. McClendon received a Bachelor of Arts from LeTourneau University in Longview, Texas; a Political Science Certification from the University of Texas at Tyler; a Master's in Theological Studies and earned a Doctorate of Ministries from Perkins School of Theology at SMU in Dallas, Texas. In addition, he was an Adjunct Professor of Religion at Jarvis Christian College in Hawkins, Texas.

Dr. McClendon served as a Board Member of the Marriage and Family Therapists Council and a member of the Texas State Board of Examiners. He is a certified instructor for PREP-Within Our Reach and Family Wellness through the Texas Health and Human Services Commission.

In addition, Dr. McClendon is President of the St. John District Congress and serves as a Chaplain for the Austin Police Department. He encourages men to be the "prophet, priest, provider, and protector" of their families. His love for preaching the uncompromising Word of God has gained him the notoriety of being "a Pastor with a heart for the people."

He and his lovely wife, Bernetta, founded the Maranatha Marriage & Family Ministries International to help strengthen marriages and families. They are the proud parents of five wonderful children (one deceased) and grandparents to 11 wonderfully energetic grandchildren and three great grandchildren.